11/11

P9-CES-787

A Day in the Life: Sea Animals

Shark

Louise Spilsbury

Heinemann Library
Chicago, Illinois

www.heinemannraintree.com
Visit our website to find out
more information about
Heinemann-Raintree books.

To order:
☎ Phone 888-454-2279
▣ Visit www.heinemannraintree.com
   to browse our catalog and order online.

Edited by Sian Smith, Nancy Dickmann, and
   Rebecca Rissman
Designed by Joanna Hinton-Malivoire
Picture research by Mica Brancic
Production by Victoria Fitzgerald
Originated by Capstone Global Library Ltd
Printed and bound in China by South China Printing
   Company Ltd

14 13 12 11
10 9 8 7 6 5 4 3

**Library of Congress Cataloging-in-
Publication Data**
Spilsbury, Louise.
   Shark / Louise Spilsbury.—1st ed.
      p. cm.—(A day in the life: sea animals)
   Includes bibliographical references and index.
   ISBN 978-1-4329-4003-4 (hc)
   ISBN 978-1-4329-4010-2 (pb)
1. Sharks. I. Title.
   QL638.9.S66 2011
   597.3—dc22
                              2010000921

Acknowledgments

We would like to thank the following for permission to
reproduce photographs: Getty Images pp.8, 23: dorsal
fin (Iconica/Jeff Rotman); Image Quest Marine pp.6, 14
(V&W/Mark Conlin), 15 (Kike Calve), 16 (Andre Seale),
19 (Masa Ushioda), 21 (Jez Tryner); Photolibrary pp.4
(Pacific Stock/James Watt), 5 (Imagestate RM/Peter
Scoones), 7, 23: breathe (imagebroker.net/Norbert
Probst), 7 (imagebroker.net/Norbert Probst), 9, 23: surface
(Oxford Scientific Films (OSF)/Chris and Monique Fallows),
10 (Oxford Scientific Films (OSF)/Gerard Soury), 11, 17,
20, 23: gills, 23: sense (Oxford Scientific (OSF)/David B
Fleetham), 12 (Oxford Scientific Films (OSF)/Chris and
Monique Fallows), 13 (Pacific Stock/Jim Watt), 18 (Oxford
Scientific (OSF)/Paulo de Oliveira), 22, 23: pup (Design
Pics Inc/Carson Ganci).

Cover photograph of a great white shark (Carcharodon
carcharias) reproduced with permission of Photolibrary
(Oxford Scientific (OSF)/Chris and Monique Fallows).
Back cover photograph of a dorsal fin reproduced with
permission of Getty Images (Iconica/Jeff Rotman). Back
cover photograph of a pup reproduced with permission of
Photolibrary (Design Pics Inc/Carson Ganci).

We would like to thank Michael Bright for his invaluable
help in the preparation of this book.

Every effort has been made to contact copyright holders
of material reproduced in this book. Any omissions will
be rectified in subsequent printings if notice is given to the
publisher.

Contents

Some words are shown in bold, **like this**.
You can find them in the glossary on page 23.

What Is a Shark?

whale shark

A shark is a type of fish that lives in oceans all over the world.

There are many different types of shark.

great white shark

Great white sharks live in warmer waters near land.

They hunt and kill other animals to eat.

What Do Sharks Look Like?

Great white sharks have a gray back and a white stomach.

They have a long, pointed nose, many sharp teeth, and large black eyes.

dorsal fin

side fin

A great white shark's body is long and pointed at both ends.

It has a triangular **dorsal fin** on its back and fins on its sides.

What Do Sharks Do All Day?

Great white sharks spend all day swimming.

The **dorsal fin** and part of the tail show when they swim near the **surface**.

Many sharks hunt at night, but great white sharks mostly hunt in the daytime.

Great white sharks swim around and stay on the lookout for food.

How Do Sharks Swim?

tail

side fins

A shark moves its tail from side to side to move forward.

The side fins help the shark to steer.

gill slits

When a shark swims along, water goes into its mouth and moves over its **gills**.

Gills take air from the water so that sharks can **breathe**.

What Do Sharks Eat?

Sharks catch and eat other large animals, such as dolphins and sea lions.

They also eat smaller animals such as turtles, crabs, and fish.

teeth

A great white shark has many triangular teeth in rows in its mouth.

The teeth are sharp with jagged edges to slice through bones and meat.

How Do Sharks Catch Food?

In the day, great white sharks look for animals that swim at the **surface**.

They swim up fast and catch the animal from below.

Great white sharks also use smell to find animals to eat.

They can smell a drop of blood from a hurt animal from far away.

How Do Sharks Hide?

In the daytime, animals cannot see a great white shark below them.

Its gray back looks the same as the darkness below.

side fin

Animals swimming below a great white shark cannot see the shark above them.

The shark's white stomach looks the same as the sky above.

What Are Shark Babies Like?

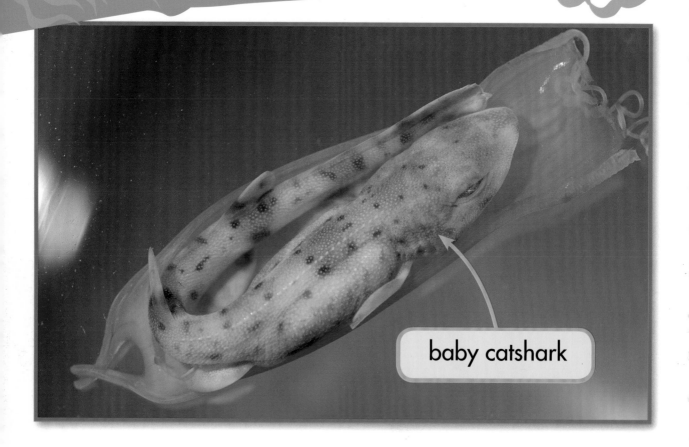

baby catshark

Baby sharks look just like their parents, only smaller.

Baby great white sharks grow from eggs inside their mother's body.

A baby shark is called a **pup**.

Shark pups leave their mother as soon as they are born.

What Do Sharks Do at Night?

Great white sharks sometimes hunt at night using a special extra **sense**.

The shark's nose can tell where an animal is moving, even if it is far away.

Nobody knows if great white sharks
sleep or not.

Some people think that sharks can sleep
and swim at the same time!

Shark Body Map

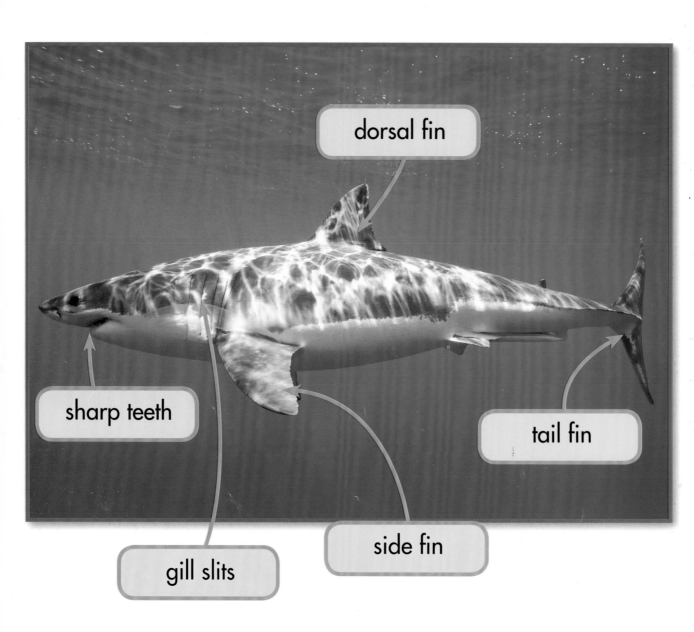

dorsal fin

sharp teeth

tail fin

gill slits

side fin

Glossary

breathe to take air into the body

dorsal fin thin, flat part that sticks up from a shark's back. Dorsal fins help sharks to keep upright in the water.

gills parts of a sea animal's body that take air from water so the animal can breathe underwater

pup baby shark

sense power that animals use to find out about the world around them, such as sight and hearing

surface top of the water

Find Out More

Books

Markle, Sandra. *Sharks* (Biggest! Littlest!). Honesdale, Pa.: Boyds Mills Press, 2008.

Nuzzolo, Deborah. *Great White Shark* (Pebble Plus). Mankato, Minn.: Capstone Press, 2008.

Websites

There are photos, fun facts, and a video about great white sharks at: kids.nationalgeographic.com/Animals/CreatureFeature/Great-white-shark

You will find information, puzzles, and links about sharks at: www.montereybayaquarium.org/efc/sharks.aspx

Index